The Hand That Rounded Peter's Dome

Also by George Drew

Toads in a Poisoned Tank (1986)

The Horse's Name Was Physics (2006)

American Cool (2009)

Bilingual Chapbook

So Many Bones (Poems of Russia) (1998)

The Hand That Rounded Peter's Dome

Poems by George Drew

Turning Point

© 2010 by George Drew

Published by Turning Point
P.O. Box 541106
Cincinnati, OH 45254-1106

Typeset in Baskerville

ISBN: 9781936370122
LCCN: 2010938580

Poetry Editor: Kevin Walzer
Business Editor: Lori Jareo

Visit us on the web at www.turningpointbooks.com

Acknowledgments

Grateful thanks to the following publications in which a number of these poems (some in earlier versions) first appeared:

The Journal of Kentucky Studies: "David and Bacchus: A Dialog," "Erasmus and Dürer: A Dialog," "The Pietà, "The Two Slaves"

Quarterly West: "Fattucci," "Febo"

Salmagundi "Julius II," "Torrigiano"

Acknowledgment is also due to Robert S. Liebert and his book *Michelangelo: A Psychoanalytical Study of His Life and Images* (Yale University Press, 1983); while I read many others along the way, this was the primary text that fueled my study of and writing about Michelangelo and the Italian Renaissance. Thanks, too, to all my fellow poets and friends who read this book in draft and offered wise counsel and very specific suggestions. Of these, particular thanks and deep and abiding gratitude go to Allen Hoey. When I faltered he pushed; when I lost hope he pushed harder; when I ran out of vision he re-envisioned me. And, as always, my humble *thank you* to my dear and patient wife Enid.

For

Mark Nepo

*He hated and was hated. He loved
and was not loved.*

—Romain Holland

Contents

A Preface	1
1475-1520	
Condivi	7
Lorenzo's Dream	10
Pico	12
Torrigiano	14
David and Bacchus: A Dialog	16
Lodovico	18
The Pietà	20
The Bookie	21
Julius II	23
Raphael	25
Leonardo	27
Bramante	29
Erasmus and Dürer: A Dialog	31
The Two Slaves	36
1520-1534	
Leo X	43
Pontormo	44
The Go-Between	48
Tommaso and Vittoria: A Dialog	49
The Blackmailer	53
Febo	54
Fattucci	57
The Sacred and the Profane	59

1534-1564

Paul III	65
The Brothers	66
The Assistant	68
Bandinelli: An Interview	69
The Final Frescoes: Paul and Peter	72
The Sisters	73
Riccio: A Dirge	75
The Nephew	78
The Funeral Book	80

A Preface

The life of Michelangelo, like his art, was turbulent. He wasn't a man at ease with himself or others. This was sometimes bad for him, but always good for biographers—good because there's a natural drama. That drama is what these poems, this book, are all about. The story, like the Renaissance, is epic, even if the poems are not. What I've tried to do is to present the essence of the story from a very human point of view. I've done this by letting the characters in the story speak—real people with real voices and unreal characters (like the statues) with invented voices. I've not refrained from sheer invention when I needed it: for instance, putting modern idioms into the mouths of long-dead people. Always my one aim was illumination of the characters and their relationships with Michelangelo, and thus illumination of the Renaissance.

The forms in which I've couched the language attempt to mirror those of the time—letters, dialogs—or, transposed on the time, contemporary forms: the interview, for example, and open forms of poetry. Michelangelo's writing of them notwithstanding, I stayed away from sonnets, mainly because the 16th Century use of them was very formal, full of elaborate conceits, which would, I thought, clash with the overall tone of the book.

I chose, from literally a cast of dozens, those characters (and works) I thought: best illustrated attitudes, were involved in central ways in Michelangelo's life, were necessary to the cross-hatching of theme and character of which the book is comprised, and served to illustrate the very human problems attending even a genius like Michelangelo.

Finally, rather than burden readers with extensive and pretentious notes, I've chosen this brief preface and a cast of characters fronting each section. Since Michelangelo's life is one of the most documented of that period, anything further would have been redundant. And the poems, I hope, tell their own stories.

I hope that what's here will act as catalyst to others, turning them to the Italian Renaissance and the wonderful cast of rogues and heroes who for one brief moment lit the minds of men with the possibility of their own grandeur.

1475 - 1520

Characters

Condivi, Ascanio: the contemporary biographer of Michelangelo.

Pico, Giovanni della Mirandola: a truly brilliant young Platonist who was a member of the Medici circle during the time Michelangelo was living and studying in Lorenzo's household.

Torrigiano, Pietro: a senior student of Lorenzo's school of sculpture in the gardens of San Marco. He punched Michelangelo in the nose, disfiguring him for life.

David and Bacchus: two of Michelangelo's early sculptures.

Lodovico: Michelangelo's father.

The Pietà: the famous one, in St. Peter's.

The Bookie: an invented character detailing an event that supposedly was real. There is no question that Michelangelo and Leonardo disliked each other.

Julius II: Guiliano della Rovere, pope 1503-13, who is responsible for the Sistine Chapel frescoes. Without doubt one of the most awesome patrons, and luckiest, of all time. His relationship with Michelangelo was turbulent and is legend.

Raphael, Sanzio: the great painter, a contemporary of whom Michelangelo was unjustly suspicious and jealous.

Da Vinci, Leonardo : the Renaissance Man of all time, of whom Michelangelo was jealous. Each represented a different approach to art and intellect.

Bramante, Donato: the great architect, whom Michelangelo suspected of plots against him to win Raphael ascendancy in the papal court.

Erasmus and Dürer: the philosopher and the painter.

The Two Slaves: sculptures of Michelangelo's, 1513-14.

Condivi

I spent last night with Michelangelo,
mostly in his shop with blocks
of marble at our feet, some works
by others interspersed among cartoons,
and boards with drawings of heroic scope
propped up in every available space.

We talked, or rather he talked,
into the early morning hours
about the finer points of the Sistine
even His Holiness had missed
in his nocturnal perambulations
on the scaffolding to check the work
of this Florentine he'd made to do
God's work as God (and Julius) wished.

He elaborated with a small boy's glee
the common sources of the enterprise
so cunningly concealed by epic sweep:

God's reaching out of nothing, nothing
more than a remake of cloud formations
seen while working the Carrara pits;
the dark creating light conceived of
as fish funneling through high waves;
the graduated size of figures as

the eye rewarded its discovered skill,
its strength, its Sistine-sized acuity.

Only once did we venture out of doors
to take the air like bantam Samson's
among the corridors of stone
that flanked the road on either side,
and witness on the river's calm
the milking of the yellow moon
hanging like Delilah's nipple just
above the red bucket of Samson's mouth.

And only once did he stop talking,
as we stood before a bush burning
in the luminescence of moonlight
like the tablature of what he said
he'd dreamed: his marble-plated birth,
God's chest heaving him out of itself
as lonely as the hangman that
the first outcasts encountered
on the strength of one wrong whim.

And then, as we stood in the road,
this Daniel of the architects of beauty,
saying stone ought not to come
between two such as we,
pulled me close and touched my eyes.

With that it was a soft goodnight,
and off I went—me, Condivi—
to turn staffs into serpents as dazzling
as the statues glowing in moonlight,
ready and willing, pray God, to really
puncture stone for the first time,
to unlock the image from within.

Lorenzo's Dream

There was a bird with eye and wing
of eagle, and neck of swan.
And in its talons were the legs,
swung wide, of a nude boy, or god,
his hair blond ringlets and his head
thrown back, mouth parted, sight
turned inward, body bending, bird
curved like a shore, vast seas of air.

I knew his talent was sublime,
but who was it being carried off?
Who carrying? I was not sure.
But I am that I will not be denied.
Let us say that the naked boy,
who signifies unprotected gifts,
has for his overseer the bird,
protector of its master's interests.

So in a fortnight Michelangelo
will come to live with me at court.
To you, the father of this prodigy,
I give my pledge that he shall sit
beside me, put above even my own
and all others of true bloodline.
And for you a job—your choice.

It is done. Oh, and Buonarroti, remember: be diligent, not poor.

Pico

Letter, 1490

My Dear----------,
                    This young boy I have told
you of is everything I'm not: unlearned,
insensitive of speech, inquisitive of nothing
but a chisel plying stone, perhaps some paint,
and even in his stature blunt, ill-formed,
with black hair, eyes not quite defined in hue,
and teeth like the unfinished lumps of stone
he hammers at with the abandon of the damned.
As is my wont, normally I wouldn't bat an eye
in his direction. But Lorenzo praises him.
And where Lorenzo looks is value, rest assured.
So I looked, too. And here is what I found:
a sibyl in the manner of the ancients carved
from marble he had gotten, so I'm told,
from masons in the garden, begging them
with charm no one, not even I, would guess
exists beneath that rough exterior of his.
There's diamond there, in need of only
the sure jeweler's hand of Time
to shape it to a gem fit for a Medici,
or even—and I don't exaggerate—a pope.
Trust me: this young boy's going to be a god

creating gods. The spark he carries in
his fingertips bespeaks a greater fire within.
And like Prometheus he'll serve and master it
at once, both Beauty's henchman and her king.
I almost pity him the torment he will know.

Torrigiano

At first it was all olive trees and light
in Lorenzo's garden where we had been
turned loose to play, shaping clay
like little towheaded gods and aping
the great masters—Donatello! Masaccio!
Lorenzo came to look upon our work,
encourage, cajole, plead. One day
he stopped by Buonarroti who
was polishing the head of a Greek faun
he'd made from marble begged
from the masons. "Good, my boy!" he said.
Good! A stupid faun fawning stupidly,
that's all it was. And Buonarroti,
puffed like a frog about to drown us all
in its bassoon of croaks. How he rubbed
my nose in the soil of his "success"!
One morning I'd had quite enough,
thank you, and turning from my sketch
I punched him in the nose so hard
the cartilage and bone crunched like a foot
on gravel. Ah! You should have seen
the disbelief that crossed his Tuscan face.
Of course the pain put paid to that,
and on the ground he went, his wails
previewing those to come for *Il Magnifico*.
So you see, although I've not seen him

again, until he leaves this dismal vale
he carries always what he learned from me.
Let me tell you, he might not soar like a bird
above us mere mortals, but his beak is bent!

David and Bacchus: A Dialog

David

It was himself he carved, not me.
You can see it in the *contrapposto* pose,
the strong but half off balance cast
of my body, in my huge right hand,
and in the tense turn of my head,
my left hand ready with the sling,
and in my tight lips and fixed eyes.
And oh! the nakedness, both mine
and his, before the moment of the kill,
the scent of giant's blood in our nose,
our neck veins swollen, stomach taut.
He carved me as he might have done
that statue of snow for Piero, full
of winter yet receptive to the Florence sun.
So, rabble, pelt me with your stones.
You cannot hurt what he has made
of his confusions, not this one.
He came from winter, and to winter he returns.

Bacchus

Easy for you to say, but look at me,
this masterpiece—his first. Dear Zeus!

What's noble in this *contrapposto* pose?
Look at my open mouth, slack as the skin
of an old man, those rolling eyes,
most likely bloodshot from the wine
of that now empty cup, those silly grapes
in my hair, and, worst by far,
the thick rotundity that once upon a time
was a stomach harder than Achilles' shield.
And that flayed skin—no tiger, that.
If, as they say, it is an emblem
of some plight of his, I'd rather less
of him, thank you, and more of what
I know I ought to be: a god, like Zeus.
Let's have a little fire and thunder,
darkness, orgies, and the eating of raw flesh!
If he's of winter, then to winter I belong.

Lodovico

Letter, undated: 1506?

My Boy,
          I have been to see that statue,
David, in the piazza. Now I see
to what a wrong pass you have come.
You write whatever you have done you did
solely to aid your family. Is this it, then?
Spending yourself in carving naked men?
A grown man, and still you pass the days
making sweat and marble dust. You should
be wed, have children, a good trade.
But, no, you'd rather chisel stone
into these mad perversions—naked men,
their cocks on view to all the world.
Why do you never chisel girls?
I think you had your way too much.
I should have used the strap more
than I did. I should have made you what
I know you could have been: a man
of letters, like Alighieri or Boccaccio.
God pardon us. God pardon *you*—and me.
I take full blame, your failure is my own.
If you must know, I am not well.
But I subsist. And you are welcome here.

Remember, keep your head warm. Oh,
and if you must carve stone, my boy,
then carve—carve *girls*!
> As Ever,
>
> Papa

The Pietà

Mother, have you looked on this masterpiece?
Seen how you hold me as you did when I
was but a child? Here joy has been
exiled, and sorrow set upon the throne.
You will not see it on your perfect brow
draped by its kerchief. Nor on your firm chin,
nor in your inward-looking marble eyes,
nor even in my horror-riddled shape
draped like a smock across your lap.
Now do you see it? There—in your left hand:
the fingers splayed like broken wings,
the deeply chiseled lifeline, and the blood,
or shadow, smudging palm and fingertips.
Here, mother, piety and pity are the same.

The Bookie

Gentlemen, place your bets! The Vecchio
is ready, walls prepared for paint.
I hear the cartoons have been done.
To whom will you ascribe your luck?
To Leonardo, whom the whole world knows
as Master? Or to an admitted prodigy,
our Michelangelo? Choose carefully:
the wisdom of experience, or fire of youth?
Can any doubt that Leonardo, nearly
twice his rival's age, is genius given flesh?
Grace issues from his very fingertips!
Likewise, dare any question Michelangelo?
Lest you doubt, consider what occurred
just recently: asked by a group
of young men arguing about some passages
from Dante to resolve the issue, Leonardo,
who was walking by, accepted their request
and joined them. Seeing Michelangelo,
and aware, as is the whole of Florence,
of that young man's expertise
in matters Alighieri, he suggested
young Buonarroti was the one to ask.
It seems that Michelangelo, no doubt
misreading scorn for praise, advised
that Leonardo, who had failed to cast
a horse in bronze, and whom the fools

had trusted all those years, do it himself.
Imagine, a man whom all the world accords
its praise addressed in such a scornful way.
Leonardo, though he uttered not a word,
nearly turned to stone himself.
So let there be no doubt: fire
is the stuff of which this young man's made.
Whether or not it will translate to
a great mural in the Vecchio, who can say?
So draw the odds yourselves, and place
your bets. *What?* 20 ducats? 20, you say!
An outrage! Blasphemy! You swine!

Julius II

I admit it. More than once I nearly
lost my way. Doubt, ambition, anger, love.
Those were the real enemies of Rome,
not the Turk nor the Spaniard nor the Gaul;
next to those they were child's play.
And as for Buonarroti, that emblazoned soul,
terribilità whose only brides were stones,
cartoons and paint—he was my weapon,
though he didn't know it, secret agent
of the Lord, *in secula seculorum*, stone
designed for shaping. Proud as stone.
(But I always called him Son.) Even I,
Guiliano, Pope and Shepherd to His Flocks,
the Vicar of His Church, etc., walked
on lamb's feet when entering the sacristy
of his imagination. Do you follow me?
I ask you, where would he—and Raphael,
Bramante and the rest—have been
without the flog of my devotion
on his back: four years of the ungiving wood
of scaffolding his table and his bed,
the ceiling his Delilah waiting for a chance?
I have made not just my own bed,
but the artisans, the makers, of the bed.
And the architecture keeps to principles
of square and circle: Leonardo's flush

Euclidics wedded to the *chiaroscuro* that
is Buonarroti's soul and gentled to a Greek-
like grace under the hands of Raphael.
My glory is that I was artist, too,
and they, especially my haunted Florentine,
the masterpiece of my studio.

Raphael

Buonarroti, sprawling in the piazza,
says he didn't like the bastard.
Last year, in that chateau,
that bastard said of Buonarroti
that he didn't like the bastard.
Where the trouble started
was in Venice, circa fifteen-five,
when a mirror free of distortion
was perfected. Nothing's been right
since, not even here in Rome,
and certainly between those two,
who have always liked to look
in mirrors: in, that is, surfaces
free of all reflections save those
of their own devising. Even
His Holiness was modest by comparison.
Buonarroti, I know for a fact, sat
for a week in the mountains near
the quarry pits staring at clouds
until he recognized the Lord
reaching out, he says, to Adam.
But we all know who that Adam was!
I never would have done the Ceiling,
I admit it. I know my limitations,
and I *do* have a kind of genius.
But I'm not one of those titans

whose vision always is so bulky,
weighed down like a bear in spring
by all that fur when it emerges,
stubborn Idea grumbling into life,
the stone chips falling to the side
of the pure figure, perfect nude.
Truly, I grew weary of their epic
bickering. What can one think of men
who think women are machines
made strictly for their pleasure,
or who don't think of them at all?
Or of much else except their fingertips?
Still, one sees harmonies. I'd rather
I were Christ positioned center
of the storm than Judas lurking
on the fringes, rather I were Samson
chained in the middle of the columns
than one of the columns. I'd like
to think that what is dampening
the Roman dust at Buonarroti's feet
is tears, not sweat. And besides,
someone has to do the invocations.

Leonardo

My Dear Donato,
                Salutations from Cloux.
These Gauls certainly are a moody lot,
much like their weather. How I miss
Milan—those golden mornings of our art.
And further back sweet Florence and Verrocchio.
Youth mixed like colors: daring, sure.
I know our countrymen consider me aloof,
but as you know, Donato, I was not so always.
Once I raced like Hermes on the wind.
And if I am a victim of the spleen's dark hues,
well, who can help it these days anyhow?
What Savonarola hath begot let no man put
asunder…. Dark days truly, friend.
But I am rambling, am I not? To cases, then!
Here is my thought: the Sistine *is* true art,
I give it that. An epic sweep it has.
And oh! the ache of being on those boards
for three long years! For that alone
he merits plaudits and a fattened purse.
The color's glorious, the theme's divine;
the grandeur of the whole incomparable.
May I say it? It is his masterpiece,
one of the treasures of our time. There now,
it's out. Da Vinci lauds our Michelangelo!
That maddening, insufferable Florentine!

And now to blows. Like any work of art
that stretches to a higher breaking point,
a place from which the solar-stricken wings
accord their Icarus a longer tumble to the sea,
its very essence is its nemesis. All that
substratum of Platonic platitudes:
Man, the Passionate! Man, the Artificer! Man,
the Lord of Reason! Man, the Teacher's Pet of God!
The *chiaroscuro* covers cracks, but they remain.
What he most needed was a hand lighter
than his. Raphael's perhaps. Or yours.
His vision started from above when where
it should have started was below
with the things of this world. God's glory
is resplendent more in little things: a blade
of grass exploding in the light, seashells
deposited like arks on mountaintops,
a child curled in the womb, a woman's yawn.
I do not mean to quibble, but the bird,
after its flight, must always down to earth.
In this I see the wings, but not the bird—
and he has only one winged angel in his work!
Ah yes, but what about the wealth
of detail? (I can hear you thinking this.)
Because I am, as you well know, a man
of few words, let me put it to you thus:
you know those rams' heads used as frame?
Goats would have been more apropos.

Bramante

My Dear Leonardo,
                        Raphael is dead.
And here I lie, listening to the choir of birds
outside my cell welcoming the dawn
with their witless menagerie of chirps,
sounding for all the world like boys
whose voices have betrayed them during mass.
And Buonarroti? As always, the catacombs
of his suspicious mind are vast enough
to hide the early Christians from Nero's wrath.
Plots here! Plots there! Plots everywhere!
Macchiavelli would himself be awed.
And you are right: his "vision" soars
beyond the grasp of normal mortals like myself.
Oh yes, it's true I lobbied hard
for Raphael, his sense of harmony,
his graceful touch. And I was right.
Look at the Ceiling, those foreshortened forms,
those muscular he-men, those wingless nudes.
Especially where he began, his Noah—there
you see the unsure dabbling of the amateur.
He even had to wipe away what he had made
and start again. What did he know of paint?
By the time he got to the Creation
he had mastered it, I grant him that.
But what about the integration of the whole?

And can we all ignore the visionary fire
of this gargantuan? Yes, he is right—
I lobbied hard for Raphael, and lobby hard
I would again. He is a sculpting man,
this master sculptor of all Italy, and in
the sculptor's workshop is where he belongs.
I know the Pope was pleased with it,
awed even, as he did himself admit.
Who wouldn't be with such extensive proof
of his own worth? But I insist:
under Raphael's sure hand
he would have still had all of that,
but with an airy blend of *spiritus*.
I lobbied hard for Raphael, but there
was never any plot. And as for all
that stuff about Sebastiano, pure rot.
Look to the Ceiling for the final proof
of what I say. You see those nudes
holding the bronze medallions? What
purpose have they? Twenty of them, no less!
He is a master, Buonarroti—of pure ornament.

Erasmus and Dürer: A Dialog

Dürer

I understand you were in Italy
just at the moment of their argument?
The Pope and Michelangelo, I mean.

Erasmus

Yes, in Bologna, I believe. And you?
Weren't you in Venice once?

Dürer

Quite so, but years before your stay.

Erasmus

Did you meet him then? Rumor has it so.

Dürer

Alas, though he passed through
the City of Canals while I was there
we did not chance to meet. And you?

Erasmus

I was in Rome but briefly,
at the time that Raphael
was painting the Pope's rooms,
and did not chance upon the man.

Dürer

To come so close, and yet to miss.
A pity, isn't it? Such a great man.

Erasmus

Great, yes. But I have no regrets.
I do not like his pagan bent.

Dürer

Ah, but the fire, good sir! The fire!
It's very nearly German—all
that passion. You see it in his nudes.

Erasmus

I see the passion, and a dismal lack
of all restraint. A little harmony
is what is needed—Reason's light.

Dürer

You mean like that in Raphael?

Erasmus

Yes, Raphael. I distrust pedestals—
whether for kings or subjects glorified
beyond their place in Nature's scheme.

Dürer

Yet Raphael paints as well.
And glorifies the beauty of our kind.

Erasmus

Yes, but within true human bounds.

Dürer

And what, pray tell, are those?

Erasmus

Why, look at the *Athens*.
On one side is Plato and his band,
and on the other Aristotle's ilk.

There is a perfect blend,
a harmony, like hot and cold,
of the emotions and the mind.

Dürer

Like the two *Captive Slaves*?
Like the *Creation* and the *Flood*?

Erasmus

Yes, his work shows it, too.
And no man loves God more,
I give you that. And yet,
there is throughout his work
a fascination with the underside
of feelings—passion ready to let go,
burst through the fetters of restraint
into expressions of pure sense
divorced from the advising mind.
He likes the nude a bit too much.

Dürer

Perhaps, but not to recognize
the ocean beating at the bottom
of even the sturdiest ship
is to invite that which you fear.

Michelangelo may like the nude,
but much as one likes wood
between oneself and the ocean.
For him, the flesh reveals the truth
of oceans both without and -in.

Erasmus

True, sir. Yet let us not forget
what I have heard that Leonardo said:
Beware, that as you try to make
your nude show all of what it feels
you don't end as a wooden man of paint.
And to that he might have added sense.

Dürer

And wasn't it you, sir, who said
of Holbein's painting of yourself
that were you really that becoming
then you wouldn't lack a wife?

Erasmus

In truth, I did.

Dürer

Indeed.

The Two Slaves

Dying Slave

Though I am standing, I'm at rest.
Though I am fettered, I'm yet free.
So take your pick: did he make me
Art sleeping after Guiliano's death?
Or Art awakened by that peerless pope?
Confusion is the stuff of art like his.
You see how my arm holds my head,
my closed eyes, and my jutting leg?
You see my polished, supple nakedness?
I'm wonderfully relaxed, and yet near death.
And you who would rejoice that life
as yet is clearly separate from death,
look again upon the beauty of my head,
one of the few he ever did, and think
on this: I live forever. What of you?

Rebellious Slave

I, too, am contradictory: Art freed
from its imprisonment by that same pope,
or Art forever fettered by his death.
But there the likeness ends. Unlike
my sleeping friend, I'm not so nice

to look upon: these straining arms,
this hard, contorted body, cracks
across my shoulder and my cheek,
the look of hardship on my stony face.
And if I'm not Art imprisoned, like
Sebastion or the figures in *Laocoön*
I clearly am the spirit fighting it.
As our wise maker said, no one
who by himself is bound can himself free.
So what is it to be? Forever sleep, or free?

1520 - 1534

Characters

Leo X: Giovanni de' Medici, pope 1513-21, son of Lorenzo and an important patron of Michelangelo.

Pontormo, Jacopo: a young, gifted artist who came under Michelangelo's sway so thoroughly that he relinquished his talent and personality to the extent that he locked himself in the choir of San Lorenzo and spent eleven years aping the Sistine Ceiling, fluctuating between his own identity and that of Michelangelo.

The Go-Between: an invented character.

Tommaso di Cavalieri and Vittoria Colonna: the two great loves of Michelangelo's life.

The Blackmailer: Pietro Aretino, the first journalist of Europe in the muckraking sense. He wielded enormous influence and power and, after ingratiating himself to artists of stature, would demand payment of their works or threaten them with ruin. It did not work with Michelangelo, despite a series of really nasty letters.

Febo di Poggio: one of the young boys Michelangelo was enamored of who seems, for his part, to have been enamored of Michelangelo's fame and finances more than of the artist himself. "The Dreamer," as Febo says, is a sketch.

Fattucci, Giovan Francesco: a chaplain who was Michelangelo's contact in the papal court during Clement's papacy. He remained one of the master's most trustworthy advocates and friends. The story of the colossus is true.

The Sacred and the Profane: the title refers to the two drawings of Tityus and Ganymede, though here I apply the Sacred to the figures carved from the stones and the Profane to the stones themselves.

Leo X

Because I didn't know what use to put
the likes of Leonardo to, and thus let him
go off to France, I am blamed. It's true.
What did I know of painting? Or of stone?
Yet everyone knew that Michelangelo
and Leonardo, had he stayed in Rome,
would have been waging war at every chance.
Was even their art worth such a price?
And, too, there was my health:
not happy in the best of times. And as
for Michelangelo, and my supposed abuse
of him, next to Julius I was grace itself!
A palm in which he rested like an egg.
And since he kept most of the time
to Florence, or the quarry pits, he was
mostly a famous name to me. There was,
I admit, the issue of the pits themselves.
It's true I made him use the ones
at Serravezzo, but that seemed intelligent,
since he was to work in Florence anyhow.
But it was *he* insisted he would oversee
the quarrying, the building of the road—
everything. And he would not be moved.
A lion I may not be, but neither am I mule.
I let him have his way. Remember that.

Pontormo

Ha! Ha! I have them now—
there's Eve, there's Adam, Noah too.
And there's the Last Judgement.
Eleven years, locked in this cold,
cursed Hell they call the Choir.
Eleven years, more than his four.
Eleven years of plaster, paint.
Of ache and weariness. Of *these*,
the children of my brilliance.
Hark! You hear the echo of the feet
approaching? Julius, come to see.
Yes, Holiness, it's I, Michelangelo.
You wish to climb the scaffold?
Here. Your hand. Give me your hand.
Les petite artistes. That's French,
you know. Which shows of what
noble stuff I'm made. Yes, yes,
as I have always kept the secrets
of my chisel as I worked,
admitting no one into my workshop
until the stone was served,
so I have the secret that it's you
who are the solid base on which
the statue of my talent rests.
Nobility is modesty in fancy dress.
Take Topolino, the stone cutter

from Cararra who always, when
shipping marble blocks to me
in Florence or in Rome,
made certain to include his own
fine figures. Once, when I
complained the legs were far
too short he cut them off and gave
to Mercury a pair of boots!
I lauded him…. Pontormo who?
Oh, *that* untutored one.
A wastrel, Holiness, and very ill,
I've heard. Too ill to be of use.
But better you beware the serpents
close at hand: Bramante, Raphael.
Beware those who say they are friend.
Look there. You see the stew of misery
I've concocted? Look to the right,
to Charon and his boat so stuffed
with scurvy souls they seem as one.
All flesh a single color tone.
Beware, beware of all of them,
and know the castings of the snake.
Consider, Holiness:
Lorenzo dead, the French dead set
on death. *Get out of Florence now!*
Go to Bologna! So I fled,
thanks to the dreams I'd had
and to the friend to whom I'd told

the dream. *Go! Go!* he said. *Get out!*
Lorenzo, dressed in nothing but
black rags, appeared and said
to warn Piero of his coming doom.
You see Piero? There he is—
among the throng of pagan damned.
Of course, I am a man who sees
that dreams are not real things,
and so I didn't say a single word
to family or friends. I simply quit
my home without a by-your-leave.
What! Afraid? You think I was afraid?
Is Adam fearful of his birth?
Look how he reaches out to God.
Afraid? Of Piero de' Medici? That,
who had me sculpt but once,
and that a simple man of snow!
Would such as that take heed?
Snakes! Snakes! O Your Holiness,
they hiss like Satan in your ear
of Michelangelo. No, no. He kept
his silence, turned and ran.
And when Lorenzo reappeared,
dressed in the same black rags,
he struck me with his staff,
his eyes like burned-out worlds,
like those of God—up there,
in the Creation of the Sun and Moon.

Do you not like it, Holiness?
Hello. Pontormo, that's my name.
Well, yes, I said to him
with sympathy: *But, really, there's
not too much drama there,
unless of course papa was cruel
and inconsiderate to her
before she died when you were six
and left you stashed inside
the dim wits of papa's dim brain.*
And I told him I remember mine,
how at seventy or so he still
could get it up like Charon's oar.
And Michelangelo, I said,
imagine the possibilities: him,
with his proud staff
parting the blue-gray waves
of his wife's long-sagging flesh,
then in the eerie pall of light
gliding like mama's dream prince
from the meadow of her bed
and into one more day of living dead.
And her still lying there
in the half light hoping to God
it was the dream itself was real.
I ask you, when you struck
Michelangelo did I strike back?
Ha! Ha! I have him now. Pontormo who?

The Go-Between

My Dear Tommaso,
                I have heard from him.
Though he's in Florence he's still here,
chained like Tityus to the vulture
of the passion tearing at his guts.
Escape is not attemptable—look
at those giant wings, those claws
clasping him to the spiral of ascent!
So far he's lost some twenty pounds,
and matched them with as many years
in six short months. He wants to know,
of you that is, which should he hunger for:
the fearsome fires of Hades burning so
profanely in his loins? Or else
the sacred but not worldly press
of spirits intertwined like Dante and his love?
Young friend, please choose. There is
much more at stake than lovers here.
And do remember, once he comes to Rome,
that is to say to you, to Florence he
will never go again.
                In Haste,
                        Your Friend

Tommaso and Vittoria

Vittoria

On Sundays when we met at San Silvestro
overlooking Rome he spoke of you
as *Cinquecento* light, the paragon of all the world.

Tommaso

And after you were laid to rest he said
his one regret was that he hadn't kissed
you on the face or brow as he had done
your hand when you lay on your bier.

Vittoria

For you there was that famous pun:
"I am held prisoner by an armed Cavalier."

Tommaso

For you the drawing of the crucifix
that crucified all others that you ever saw.

Vittoria

Through love alone comes proof of that
which is beloved. Do you agree?

Tommaso

Indeed. He was in love with love.

Vittoria

"The good I pledge myself, bad I reject."

Tommaso

And yet the viciousness persists.
So many nudes, they say.
And most of men.
They even speak of impotence.

Vittoria

Yes. As he wrote upon my *Pietà*:
"They think not of the blood it's cost."

Tommaso

Was ever any man so chaste?

Vittoria

Those so disposed see truth
where there is only what they think.

Tommaso

And as he wrote me once, he could
as well forget his need for food
as the name of one he loves.

Vittoria

"Weighed down by years and filled with sin,"
as he once put it in his verse,
how could he find the room for more?

Tommaso

Food fires the body, love the soul.

Vittoria

And love for you made his soul blaze.

Tommaso

And you, as he once said, a man or god
speaking inside a woman's flesh.

Vittoria

I was no man or god, merely a woman
loving him who was a god speaking
inside a woman masquerading as a man.

Tommaso

And I a man in love with the same god.

Vittoria

God bless this god.

Tommaso

Amen.

The Blackmailer

Often, as I stood looking up
at that great sweep of color, I
wondered what it must have been like
being there on those boards,
paint dripping in his beard,
eyes going bad, arms aching,
neck like a ribbon tied in knots.
And then I knew: it's like
having your lover riding you.
At first it's fun, then ecstasy,
then agony as she gets close
but will not…will not come.
But then I thought again,
and then the image came undone.
What if the lover is a boy?

Febo

Letter to Aretino, undated

Dear A,
       To them all I am a curiosity,
at odds with all the others—
Andrea, Gherado, Antonio, Tommaso.
Whereas they have beauty of the body
and of the head, I've body only.
But because I cannot spell
does not mean I cannot see.
Good breeding's nothing but
a fancy landscape blocking its own view.
And what do I, once an apprentice
of bad breeding to the one
my betters say sees everything,
see? I see, for one,
they think this whitebeard bird
in sculptor's dress scorns all
the normal appetites. Sir,
I could tell you things
and show you letters, would
make even your cheeks red.
Mind you, I'm not affirming
this or that—no man was ever
more forthcoming than this one.

Money was no consideration,
ducats were mine as much
as his—although I had
to urge him, after his retreat
to Rome, not to fail me
in recompense, if not of purse
then heart, for special services
(in his workshop, you understand).
Yet there are stress-cracks
in the best of armaments.
Look at this odd sketch—
a present, as he said,
for one so like a son.
Son indeed! Never mind
naked Gabriel with his horn;
never mind the several heads
in the box; never mind the ball
on which the giddy god reclines.
Look instead at that circle
of sin—those writhing beasts,
those fornicators, those hard cocks
about to rend the Eden
of a woman's thighs—
and on that one, whose hand
is gnarled and tough, so like
the chunk of a half-sculpted stone.
"The Dreamer," he calls it.
Well, sir, I see the dream,

and I know who is the dreamer.
And should we turn like a pillow
every dream, what have we then?

                              Yours,
                                    Febo

PS: Please know, I offer these
      without thought of reward;
      and should you so insist,
      whatever you do judge
      as fit and proper recompense,
      is thought of, humbly, as a gift.

Fattucci

Elegies! Elegies! My better angels try
to cheer me, but all I can think of
is stark colors, blacks and whites,
earthen rusts and reds and browns
like those now settling into the Sistine,
the sap slowing beneath the limbs,
showing the more the leaves intone
of God's beneficence—and his.
Let's not forget how he desired
to sculpt a mouse upon his *Day!*
Then, too, his letters always spoke,
beneath their antic give and take,
of how the passions and their works
decay, of how the stone will crack.
Take Clement, that poor man who left
his flock the poorer for his years
on Peter's throne. Oh, how he loved
his Michelangelo! Whom Fate
had bound to him as brother,
first when they were boys together
in Lorenzo's court—bound, I say,
half in the Heaven of their innocence,
half in the Hell we call experience.
Once Clement bade me to instruct
the Master to make plans to carve
a fifty-foot colossus for the Medici,

to be positioned on the corner just
across from della Stufa's residence.
His answer came. He would, he wrote,
despite his latest plague: weak knees.
This set the tone. The barber shop
is where he said it should be placed,
seated on top and hollowed out—
even the head, which then would serve
as a dovecote or, better yet, belfry
for San Lorenzo, that the sounds
of mercy, which on feast days ring
all the more, should choir the Lord.
Honor was the last of which he spoke,
then signed himself *Your Michelangelo*.
So you see, there is a playful tone,
and there are angels in his words.
But as with the autumnal tree,
underneath the sap begins to freeze.
With banter was the pope put off;
with jests the darkest angel bound.

The Sacred and the Profane

Sacred

There are some days when the skies
above the chisel line of trees
and the palette of brown fields
exert a powerful appeal,
and we can nearly believe
we've found the final resting place
of the great bird of fire.
It's then, with flint in our eyes
of the master who has wrenched
from stone our almost unimaginable shapes,
that we rise like the great bird
into the hard seed of the sun.
And in the pyre the embers flare,
then sink into a flood of gray
those in the Valley of the Ashes
swaddle themselves in like a cloak,
sobbing as more ashes snipe at them
from the great rift of the eternal light.

Profane

Here we have lain for years on end
in Florence and in Rome, ideas

and figures locked in stone
from Seravezza and Carrara, while
the only one who can release us from
these purgatories of eternal sleep
and shape us into forms the like
of which the world has never seen
sits in his workshop writing poems
or roaming quarries for more stone
to weigh down even more this misery,
not only of ourselves who must
forever languish as mere stone,
but of our master, Michelangelo,
locked deep within his own cold stone.

1534 - 1564

Characters

Paul III: Alessandro Farnese, pope 1534-49, under whom Michelangelo did the Last Judgment painting in the Sistine.

The Brothers: Michelangelo's four siblings.

The Assistant: an invented character, but based on a young boy whom Michelangelo actually referred to as this "dunghill of a boy."

Bandinelli, Baccio: another minor sculptor who hated Michelangelo.

The Final Frescoes: those of the Conversion of St. Paul and the Crucifixion of St. Peter.

The Sisters: Rachel and Leah, two of Michelangelo's sculptures.

Riccio, Luigi del: an exiled Florentine banker, one of Michelangelo's dearest and most loyal friends who even nursed him back to health, sent him food and, on one occasion, quarrelled with him over some sonnets. He died in 1546, some said of a broken heart at the death of his young nephew, for whom he had an undoubted love.

The Nephew: Lionardo, the son of Buonarroto, to whom Michelangelo penned many letters over the years, and over whom he held absolute control, as he did over all his family.

The Funeral Book: Volterra, Daniele da, was a major artist heavily influenced by Michelangelo; VASARI, Giorgio, was the biographer of the famous *Lives of the Artists*, the last of which was that of Michelangelo, and was one of the Master's truest friends.

Paul III

As always, blame must be upon the victim
levied as much, if not more, as on him
who stands accused. While it is true
I threatened him with cancellation of the tomb
he was enamored of—alas, those Medici!—
remember, please, I'd waited thirty years
to have that Buonarroti work for me.
Remember, too, I showed him more
than papal courtesy: I dared to honor him
by going, with full retinue, into his house—
I, Pope, like some awed tourist in his studio.
I was not to be denied, not after that.
And, finally, you know how stubborn he
could be—for instance, working secretly
(oh yes, I knew) on statues for that cursed tomb.
It was blackmail, but look at the rewards
my actions reaped: two papal chapels
luminescent with his work, St. Peter's dome,
and the piazza on the Capitol. No,
I was not going to be denied by him.
Even the Lord, in His own interests
and ours, attempted to insure that men
would always travel the right path
by threatening them with hellfire.
Sometimes the slightly crooked path is best.

The Brothers

                Michelangelo! Michelangelo!

God, how we tire of the very sound
of those five syllables—sounds
that greet us everywhere we go.
He was the second of the five
our mother bore, the most vexatious
and least promising, yet the one
with angels in his fingertips. Why so?
His birth itself was hard, like stone
that is not pliant to the chisel—
due to Mama's fall from her horse
while crossing the mountains between
Caprese and Florence. She spread
her legs for three more of us,
but it was his birth that did her in.
Our dear sweet mother, dead at 26—
her lovely moon-round face, dark Tuscan eyes,
soft whisper of a voice like swishing reeds.
Even now, all these years later, we can see
her face hovering like the sun above our cots,
and the warm rays of her smile lighting
the dark room in which we floated
like new planets, specks in God's black eye.
He was only six when death took her,
and most of those were spent apart:

first, at his nurse's breast taking in
the hammer and the chisel with her milk;
second, under the strict thumb of Papa,
who saw worlds for him to conquer,
but with a pen, not paint or stone.
But his remorse is proof he blames himself.
Has he ever wed? Has he sired children?
Has he a home? In all but one
of his Madonnas Mother Mary never looks
upon the child. Even in the famous one,
the *Pietà*, she looks not at her son's
death-figured face, but at the marbled
pity of his lacerated body. So,
that he could summon such resolve,
such strength of spirit as to lie for some
three years flat on his back is no surprise.
So did Mama, giving pleasure to a man
mewling in the dark with desire, and birth
to one who spends his life wet-nursing stone.

The Assistant

Just as his body, so his mind has its routines.
It rises in the early dawn still cloaked
in thoughts of workmanship, great themes
that wrap it like a snake, takes nourishment
from the anticipation of the inert lump
of stone upon which it will work its will,
reviews its rough cartoon, gathers its tools,
and joyous as the hues of Raphael
sets to, toiling through the long afternoon
to bring forth from the stubborn stone
the figure that is locked somewhere within.

Night comes and still the work goes on,
until the muscles emulate the stone
and send him off to bed and fitful rest.
The cock crows and again it all resumes.
Or, if in a rare mood, he dines with friends
and talks about the work he hasn't done,
bemoans his lack of progress, cost of stone,
impediments of fortune, and tomorrow's work.
And I? This dunghill of a boy? Either way,
I'd have to hear the birds at dawn again.
But he's kicked me out. Pure luck, I'd say.

Bandinelli: An Interview

Bandinelli is a short man, stooped by years, with not an ugly face but not one that is handsome, either. His eyes are self-contained and brown as mud along the Arno. When he speaks he does so in a quick, staccato manner, like a crow cawing from a tree. We talked one afternoon in August at his villa just outside of Florence.

Q: It is widely held that you hate him. Is this true?

A: Yes, I hate him—as he was born to be.
To do less would be insult and farce.

Q: Why so? Do you consider him duplicitous?

A: Unlike Leonardo, he projects no mask,
no tact, no charm—in short, no politics.

Q: How do you see his character?

A: His character is like his marble-
hardened hand, or like his Tuscan face:
completely unadorned. In other words,
my dear Condivi, what you see you get.

Q: If he is so ingenuous, then how explain
your actions, and, for that, your hate?

A: I simply give it back, in spades
     when I can. How else could one react
     to such a madman. And he *is* mad.
     What else to call it when he dreams
     of sculpting into human shape a rock
     the size of that between Carrara and the sea?

Q: But dreams are dreams, not fact.
     And do not all the artists dream?

A: Would such a thought occur to you or me?

Q: Can you enlighten us with one offense
     he has done you? Specifically.

A: He tried to gain the *Hercules* commission,
     which many wanted me to have.

Q: Can you elaborate?

A: You've heard the joke about the block
     of marble for the *Hercules*? How it
     fell into the Arno off the barge because
     it much preferred that kind of death
     to mauling by my hand? Such is
     the mauling *I* received at his hard hand.

Q: But did you not in fact receive the *Hercules*?

A: Oh yes. And there today he stands—
     on equal footing, I might add,
     with his huge *David*. But it cost me years.

Q: But you admit once you had it
     he never tried to wrest it back?

A: My dear Condivi, I know you like me
     just as little, but reflect on this:
     in hating him I show him true esteem,
     by giving him the only thing he knows:
     the gift of stone. What more for such a man?

The Final Frescoes: Paul and Peter

How strange that for his final strokes
of brush on plaster it is we he chose
to render: one in terror, one in pain.
In this the Lord comes down that He
might raise the struck-down up;
and in the other, one is stricken down
that he might rise to greet the Lord.
And stranger yet that in these works
is caught forever two whose worlds
have been turned upside down by one
whom the Lord sent into this world
with brush and chisel in his hands
to set things right side up again.

The Sisters

I am Leah, the active one.

    And I am Rachel, the thoughtful one.

They call us minor works.

    And we indeed are earthy, bland.

But I am more so, dressed in normal gown.

    The light of Heaven's in my lifted eyes.

The dust of mankind in my downward gaze.

    Together we are love:

of both mankind and God.

    They say we were his final finished work,

and that he was cold as the stone.

    And that is why we are so bland.

To this we say it is but just.

What else could they insist we be?

Twin suns exuding in the sight of God?

How else are we to show our love,

and therefore his,

of both mankind and God

except with modesty and calm?

My name is Rachel,
      mine is Leah,

and the good Pope Julius was correct:

our Michelangelo has won.

Riccio: A Dirge

Like me, he is dying of love.
Sometimes it slaughters him
with outright bliss,
sometimes with the detachment
of an island miles offshore.
I have nursed him, I myself
sent him cheese and wine
that he might keep his strength.
I have quarreled with him
to keep his mind off it,
but to what avail?
Like me, he is dying of love.
Love—but how can that be?
Does not he love the images
storming inside his head?
Does not he love the coasts
of ivory at the edge of touch?
Does not he love the stones'
whirlwind of chips and dust
falling on him like leaves?
Does not he love the sound
of chisel and of brush
filling his ears with more
than empty plenitude?
If, as for me, death is
a lover it is killing him.

See how he reaches out to it
between its mass of flame
and the rooted masterpiece
under his trembling hand.
This love is killing him,
yet he has perished many times
in the stony hands of men
and had his bones scattered
like barren seeds bent double
over their own thorns.
Those deaths were not friendly,
so why should this not be?
Like me, he is dying of love,
so let death come and let
death spirit him away
to the Hades of the heart.
For him death is but friendly,
and he shall burrow through
the tombstone of his misery
into the Promised Land
of all the ancient prophecies.
And with the bird of fire
he shall not have to rise
when all the ashes are as one
and storming toward the sky.
See, there his monuments
already raise him to the sun,
this Alighieri of the stone.

O double death come near!
This master fears you not,
this masterpiece, this one
you suckle at your breast.
For never, death, can you
a scabbard that is made
to hold the truest knife
make hide a crooked blade.
I, Riccio, am well content.
O my Cecchino! O my little one!

The Nephew

From the beginning we were joined
by death: his mother my great aunt
when he was six, and my papa
his brother when I was eight.
And three years later, his papa.
From then on he was more to me
than famous Uncle Michelangelo,
more than just an honored name.
He was like the stone he carved:
massive, indomitable and suffused
with a kind of supple glow
that was less than flesh
but more than stone,
a kindred hanging in between
the world he dreamed
and the world he knew.
One moment he would carp
about the cost of our insulting gift
of three coarse shirts,
then in the next breath talk
of his regard for eight new linen shirts
we'd sent to him in Rome.
To him I was a son,
and therefore had to bear
paternal liberties like a son.
He was my liege:

carping, suspicious, sometimes cruel.
But when Cassandra came
into the circle of my life
how generous he was—
gifts by the score for her,
a diamond and a ruby ring.
Anything. Anything she desired.
And when our children died
his courage shored our hearts.
Oh, far far better that you believe
it better children die before old age,
he wrote. And even though
he'd set our teeth on edge
with his ornately penned complaints
arriving once fortnightly
at our door, somehow we believed.
It wasn't hard. There *is* this *Pietà*
to which he took his sledge
and left Christ with one leg.
(He said it was because Urbino
nagged him so—the manservant
he'd nursed for five long months
as he lay dying. Letters,
though they spoke of purity,
were smudged by ink and tears.)
Of all his work, I like best this
and the *Rondanini*, their grace
and sadness. Pity and stone.

The Funeral Book

Santa Croce

Volterra

He didn't like old age. That was a lowering,
and he had grown used to heights. Even

the *Pietà*, for all the depth of agony on Mary's face,
her open hand with its full knowledge of the Tree,

her knees spread wide for her son—even there
there is a certain height, of vision and of grace.

Here is this bust of mine showing what I saw:
a sinewy sadness that transfigured everything.

Where are the heights in that fixed stare?
What vision in those tightened lips?

Here is the man Vasari knew: the one who wore
for months on end buskins of dog skin,

who in the end pulled off his own skin with them;
the one who wrote of stones and couldn't piss;

the one with palsied hands and aching joints.
Is this the sum of Buonarroti, then?

Look again: at the Greek cast of the whole,
the studied tilt toward the earth of the head,

the eyes wide open, mollified, like marble
rendered into flesh. My friends,

it is a short way back to earth but long to stars.
For this maker of giants, there were no giants

left to tame. Look to the heavens—*there!*
See how he shines? And he is cast in bronze.

Vasari

Truly, God's ways are strange. How odd,
and yet appropriate, that even at the end,

as he had often had to do when Julius sat
on Peter's throne, he left Rome on the run,

smuggled out in a bale like contraband.
But he is here at last, and so am I,

an architect in letters of his noble life;
I, who have enjoyed so many of my days

wound like a small, crooked stream
through the swollen ocean of his life.

That he approved of this is my delight.
Unlike Leonardo, who wanted to divert

the Arno, he had no desire to block
the flow of anything, except bad art.

His face was round, eyes small and dark
with yellow points and sometimes blue,

lips thin, chin good, ears big, brow square
and ample with exactly seven lines,

and hair as black as *Il Magnifico*'s.
Unadorned in body, he had radiance.

We shared sonnets and many lovely things,
but in art he was a giant and only giants

can truly fathom that. As for all of us,
only in this do we excel: that he was friend.

George Drew

George Drew was born in Mississippi and raised there and in New York State, where he currently lives. *Toads in a Poisoned Tank*, his first book, was published in 1986, and a chapbook, *So Many Bones (Poems of Russia)*, in 1997 by a Russian press, in a bilingual edition. A second collection, *The Horse's Name Was Physics*, appeared in 2006 from WordTech Communications, under their Turning Point imprint. In 2009 a third collection, *American Cool*, appeared from Tamarack Editions. Drew has published widely, with poems appearing recently or upcoming in journals around the country. His work also has been anthologized, most recently in *The Southern Poetry Anthology, II: Mississippi* (Texas Review Press, 2010). Drew has been nominated twice for the Pushcart Prize, most recently in 2010, and is the winner of several awards, such as the Paumanok Poetry Award, the *Baltimore Review* Poetry Prize, and the *South Carolina Review* Poetry Prize, and he was runner-up for the *Chautauqua Literary Journal* Poetry Contest. *American Cool* won the 2010 Adirondack Literary Award for best poetry book of 2009.